UPDATED EDITION

Guess What!

Workbook 1
with Digital Pack

CB123877

American English

Susan Rivers
Series Editor: Lesley Koustaff

CAMBRIDGE

CAMBRIDGE
UNIVERSITY PRESS & ASSESSMENT

Shaftesbury Road, Cambridge CB2 8EA, United Kingdom

One Liberty Plaza, 20th Floor, New York, NY 10006, USA

477 Williamstown Road, Port Melbourne, VIC 3207, Australia

314–321, 3rd Floor, Plot 3, Splendor Forum, Jasola District Centre, New Delhi – 110025, India

103 Penang Road, #05–06/07, Visioncrest Commercial, Singapore 238467

Cambridge University Press & Assessment is a department of the University of Cambridge.

We share the University's mission to contribute to society through the pursuit of education, learning and research at the highest international levels of excellence.

www.cambridge.org
Information on this title: www.cambridge.org/9781009798631

First published 2016
Updated edition 2024

20 19 18 17 16 15 14 13 12 11 10 9 8 7 6 5 4 3 2 1

Printed in Malaysia by Vivar Printing

A catalogue record for this publication is available from the British Library

ISBN 978-1-009-79863-1 Workbook with Digital Pack Level 1
ISBN 978-1-009-79857-0 Student's Book with eBook Level 1
ISBN 978-1-009-79864-8 Teacher's Book with Digital Pack Level 1
ISBN 978-1-107-52697-6 Flashcards Level 1

Additional resources for this publication at www.cambridge.org/guesswhatue

Contents

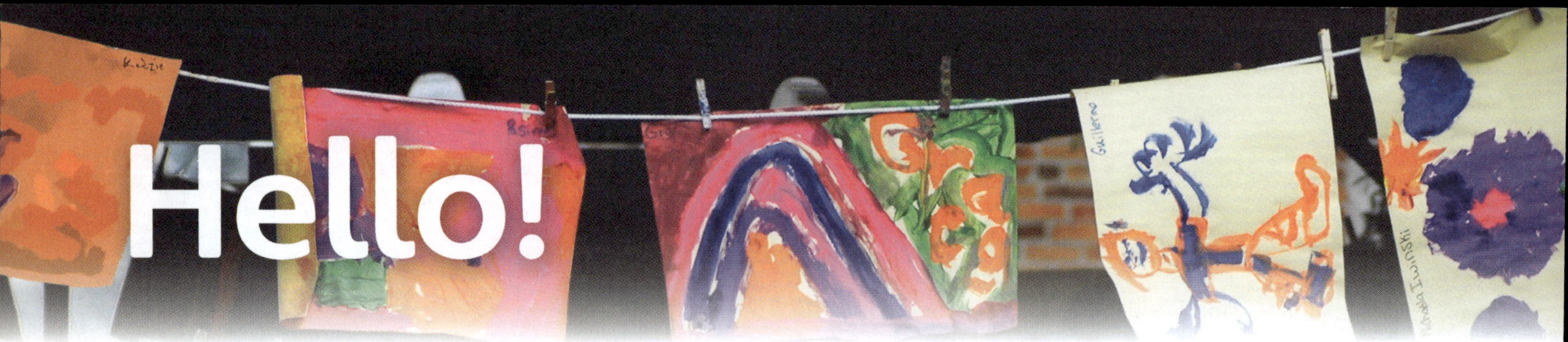

Hello!

1 Look and match.

2 Ask and answer with a friend.

1 Hello, I'm Mandy. What's your name?

2 Hello, I'm Jack.

3 This is Penny.

4 Hello, Penny.

3 0.05 Listen and stick.

4 0.06 Listen and number.

a

b

c

1

5 Think What's next? Draw a line.

1	2	4	6	2	4	6	2	4	10
2	8	9	10	8	9	10	8	9	6
3	3	5	7	3	5	7	3	5	4
4	6	5	4	6	5	4	6	5	3
5	1	8	3	1	8	3	1	8	7

6 0.09 Listen and write the numbers in the pictures.

1

2

3

4

7 0.12 Listen and color.

8 About Me Look. Then draw and say.

1

2

How old are you?

I'm …

What's your favorite color?

My favorite color's …

My picture dictionary → Go to page 84: Check the words you know and trace.

9 0.14 Listen and check ✓.

1

2

3

4

10 What's missing? Look and draw. Then stick.

11 Trace the letters.

A pink and purple panda.

12 Listen and circle the *p* words.

0.17

What color is it?

1 Listen and color.

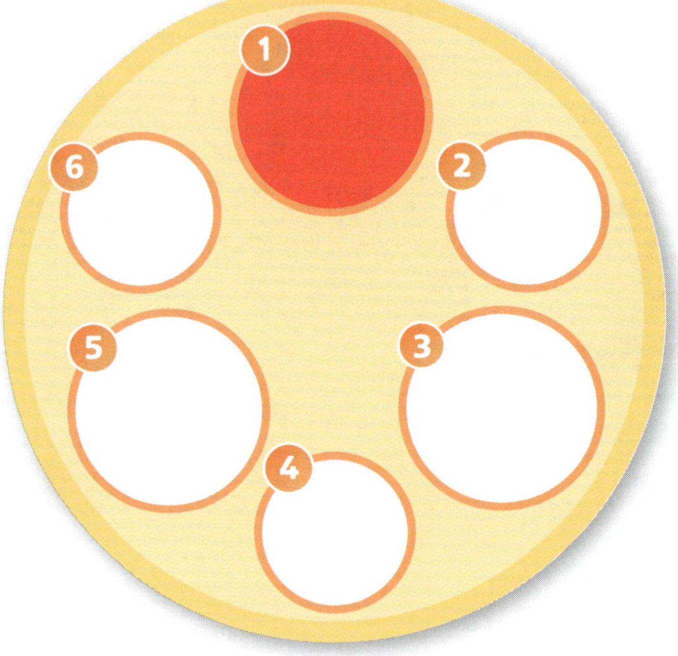

2 Look and color.

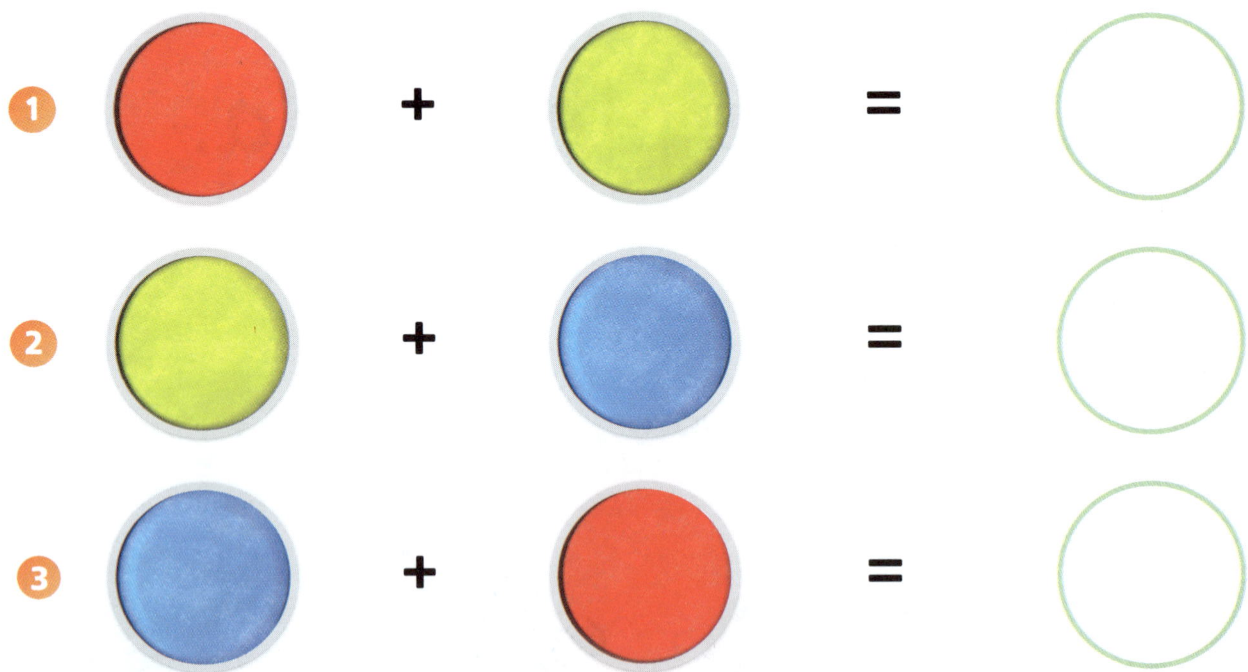

Evaluation

1 Follow the lines. Then trace and say.

a David

b Olivia

c Leo

d Tina

2 What's your favorite part? Use your stickers.

3 Puzzle Trace the color.

pink

Then go to page 93 and color the Hello! unit pieces.

1 School

1 (1.04) Listen and check ✓.

1	2	3	4
a  ✓	a  ☐	a  ☐	a  ☐
b  ☐	b  ☐	b  ☐	b  ☐

2 Look and match.

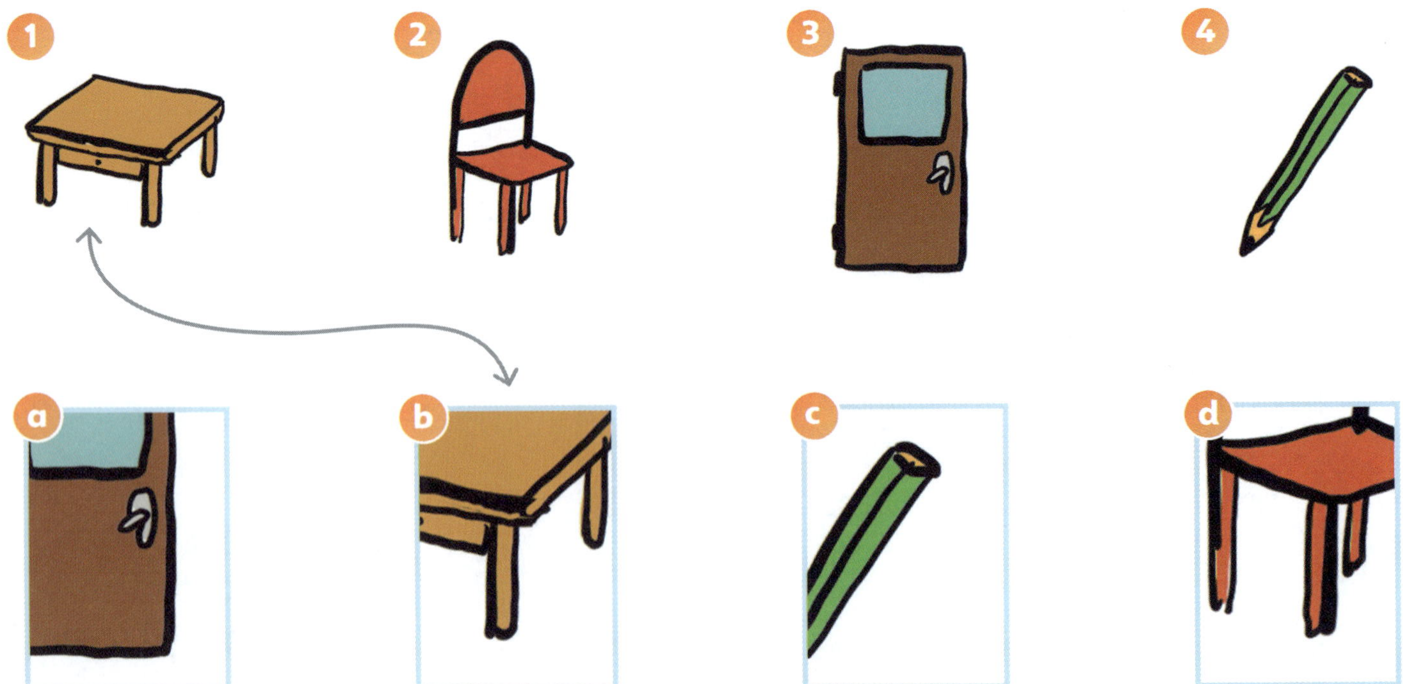

3 1.06 Listen and stick.

1

2

3

4

5

4 Think What's next? Draw a line.

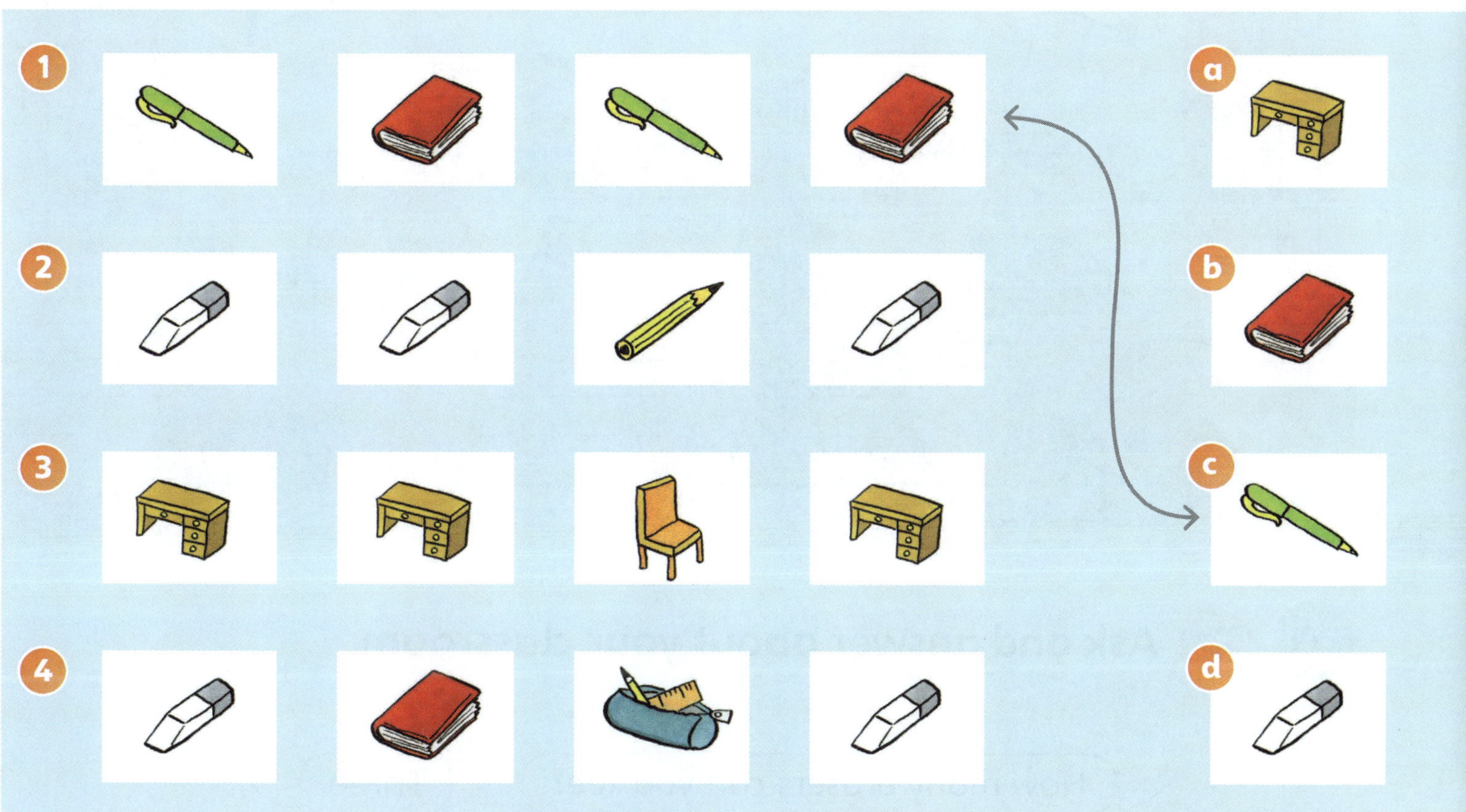

My picture dictionary → Go to page 85: Check the words you know and trace.

5 Look and count. Write the number.

2

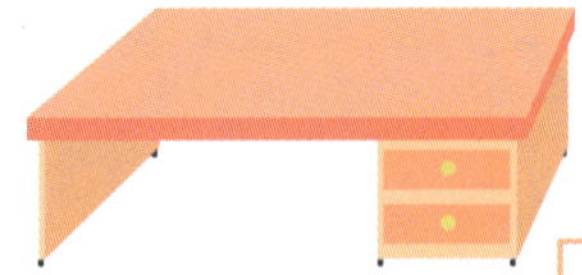

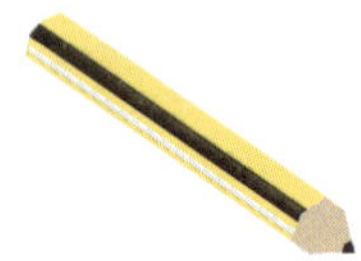

6 About Me Ask and answer about your classroom.

How many erasers can you see?

Three.

7 1.11 Listen and check ✓ or put an ✗.

1

2

3

4

8 Think Circle the different one.

1 a

b

c

d

2 a

b

c

d

9 1.13 Listen, look, and match.

1

2

3

4

5

6

a

b

c

d

e

f

10 What's missing? Look and draw. Then stick.

11 Trace the letters.

A bear with
a blue book.

12 Listen and circle the *b* words.

1.16

1 

2 

3 

4 

What material is it?

1 Look and match.

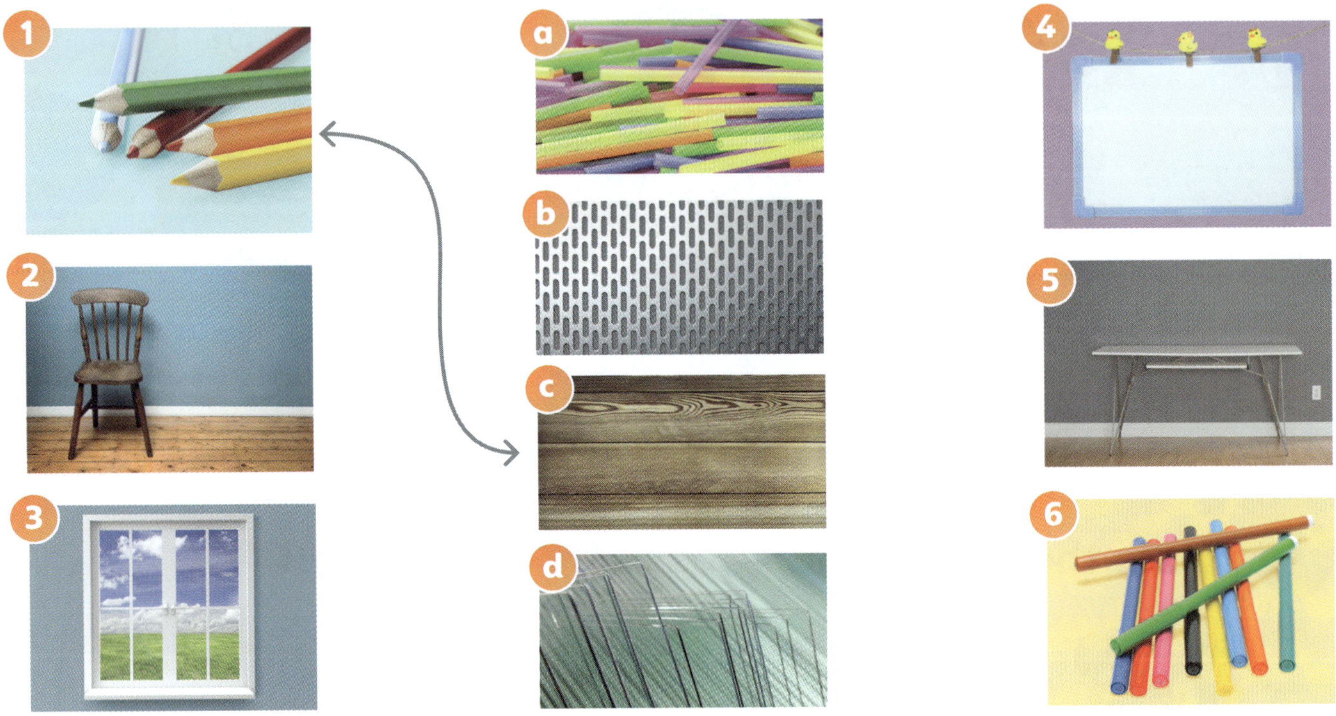

2 1.18 Listen and check ✓.

1	2	3	4
a  ✓	a 	a 	a 
b 	b 	b 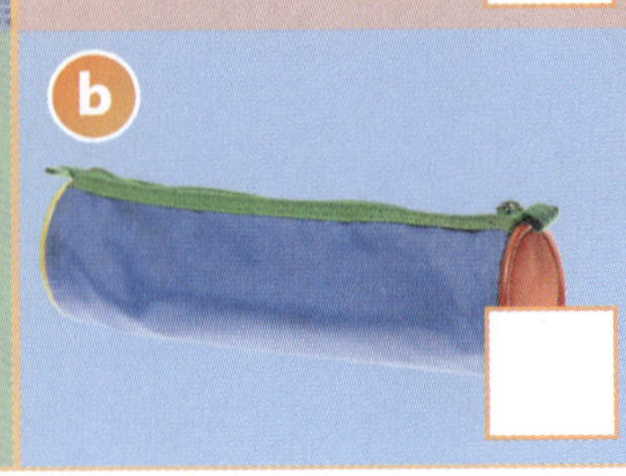	b 

Evaluation

1 Look and trace. Then say.

1

book

2

desk

3

pen

4

chair

5

eraser

6

pencil

2 What's your favorite part? Use your stickers.

3 Puzzle Trace the color.

red

Then go to page 93 and color the Unit 1 pieces.

2 Toys

1 Listen and check ✓.

1	2	3	4
a  ✓	a  ☐	a  ☐	a  ☐
b  ☐	b  ☐	b  ☐	b  ☐

2 Look, match, and say.

1 kite.

1 

2 

3 

4 

a 

b 

c 

d 

3 2.06 Listen and stick.

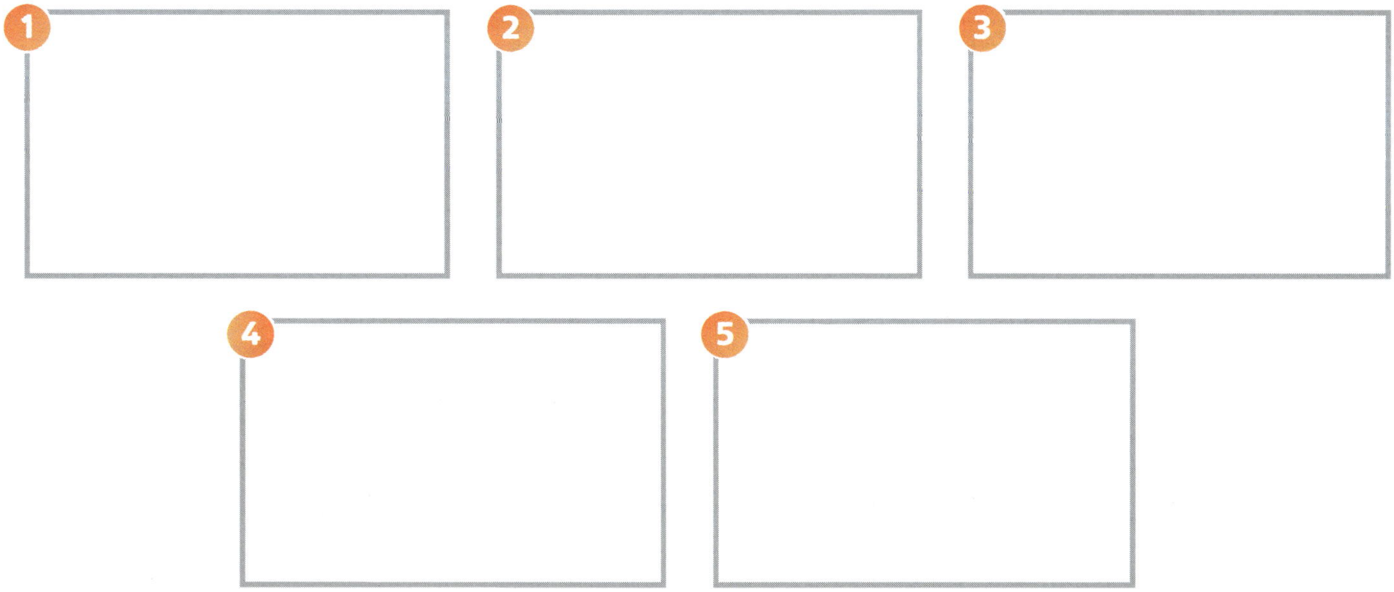

4 Think Look and circle the toys.

My picture dictionary → Go to page 86: Check the words you know and trace.

5 2.09 Listen and check ✓ or put an ✗.

1  ✓

2  ☐

3  ☐

4  ☐

6 About Me Draw your favorite toy and say.

What's this?

It's a …

7 2.11 Listen and number the pictures.

8 2.12 Listen and draw the pictures.

1	2
3	4

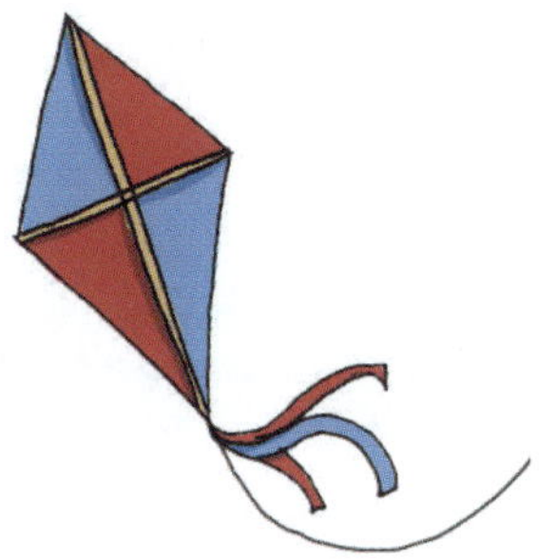

9 2.14 Listen and check ✓.

1

2

3

4

10 What's missing? Look and draw. Then stick.

a

b
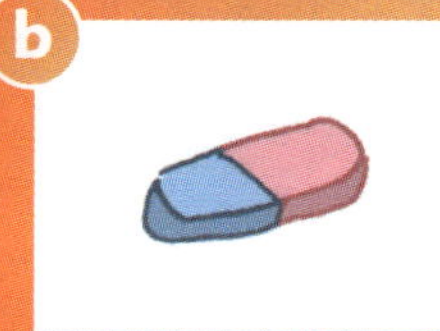

c

I'm polite.

11 Trace the letters.

A turtle with
two teddy bears.

12 2.17 Listen and circle the *t* words.

1

2

3

4

Is it electric?

1 2.19 **Listen and check ✓ (electric) or put an ✗ (not electric).**

1 
✗

2 

3 

4 

5 

6 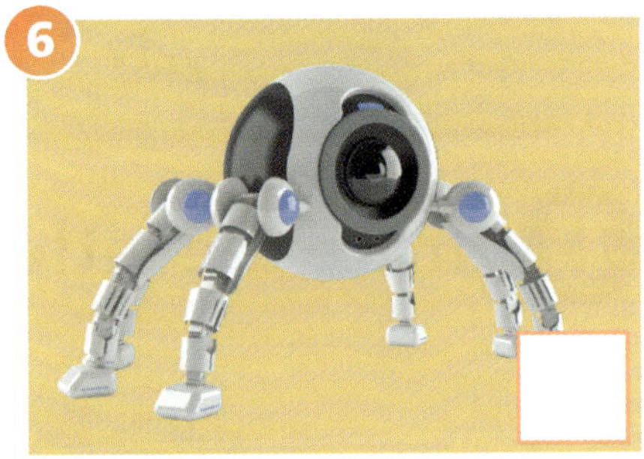

2 Look at Activity 1 and draw.

Electric	Not electric

Evaluation

1 Look and trace. Then say.

1

kite

2

robot

3

ball

4

bike

5

doll

6

camera

2 What's your favorite part? Use your stickers.

3 Puzzle Trace the color.

green

Then go to page 93 and color the Unit 2 pieces.

Review Units 1 and 2

1 Look and say. Find and circle.

2 2.21 Listen and number the pictures.

a

b

c

d

e

f

3 Family

1 Trace the words and match.

1 mom
2 dad
3 sister
4 brother
5 grandma

2 Look and write the number.

1 ~~cousin~~ 2 uncle 3 grandpa 4 aunt

3 Listen and stick.

1 ☐ 2 ☐ 3 ☐ 4 ☐ 5 ☐

4 Think Read, look, and check ✓.

1 dad

☐ ☐ ☑

2 aunt

☐ ☐ ☐

3 grandma

☐ ☐ ☐

4 brother

☐ ☐ ☐

My picture dictionary → Go to page 87: Check the words you know and trace.

5 Look, read, and match.

1 

Who's this?

2 

Who's this?

3 

Who's this?

4 

Who's this?

5 

Who's this?

a 

It's my grandma.

b 

It's my aunt.

c 

It's my grandpa.

d 

It's my dad.

e 

It's my sister.

6 About Me Draw a member of your family. Then ask and answer with a friend.

Who's this?

It's my …

7 3.11 Listen, read, and check ✓.

1

my brother ☐
my cousin ☑

2

my mom ☐
my aunt ☐

3

my mom ☐
my grandma ☐

4

my sister ☐
my cousin ☐

5

my cousin ☐
my aunt ☐

6

my dad ☐
my uncle ☐

8 Look, read, and circle the correct word.

1 Who's **this** / **that**?
It's my uncle.

2 Who's **this** / **that**?
It's my cousin.

3 Who's **this** / **that**?
It's my grandpa.

4 Who's **this** / **that**?
It's my sister.

9 3.13 Listen, look, and match.

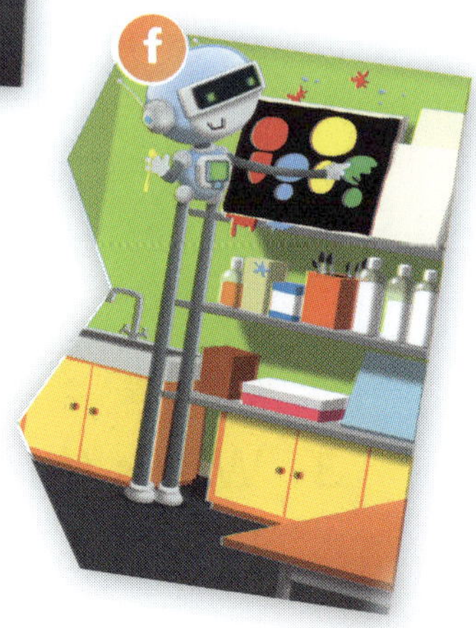

10 What's missing? Look and draw. Then stick.

11 Trace the letters.

A dolphin in
a red desk.

12 Listen and circle the *d* words.

1 

2 

3 

4 

What continent is it?

1 3.18 **Listen and write the number.**

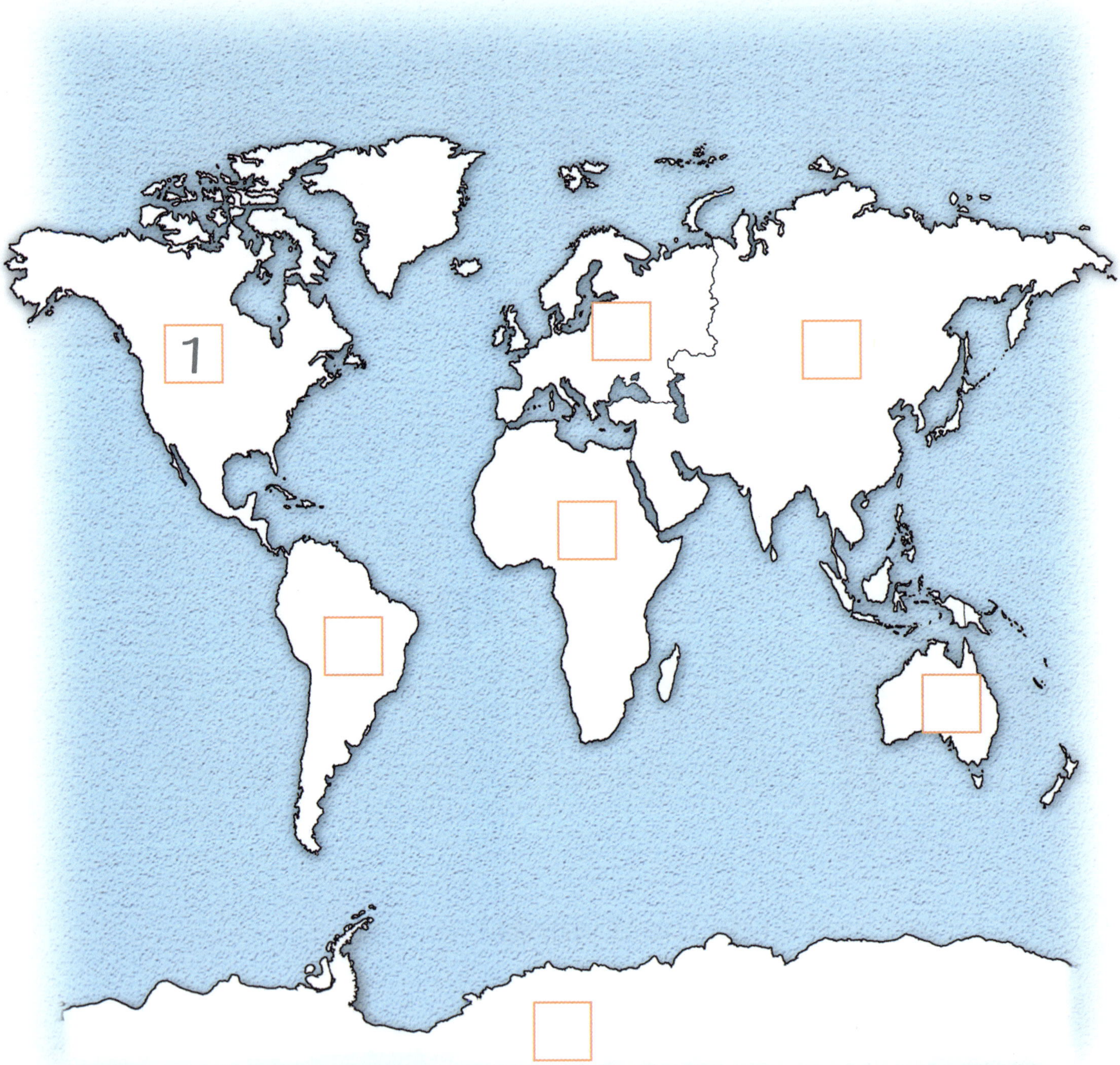

2 3.19 **Look at the map again. Listen and color.**

Evaluation

1 Read and trace. Then circle and say.

1 aunt

a b

2 grandma

a b

3 uncle

a b

4 brother

a b

2 What's your favorite part? Use your stickers.

3 Puzzle Complete the color.

o_a_g_

Then go to page 93 and color the Unit 3 pieces.

4 At home

1 Look at the picture and write the letter.

1 hallway e 2 yard ___ 3 bathroom ___ 4 dining room ___
5 apartment ___ 6 kitchen ___ 7 bedroom ___ 8 living room ___
9 balcony ___ 10 house ___

2 Listen and stick.

1

2

3

4

5

6

3 Look, read, and circle the correct word.

1 

kitchen / dining room

2 

hallway / living room

3 

bedroom / balcony

4 

kitchen / bathroom

5 

hallway / yard

6 

balcony / dining room

My picture dictionary → Go to page 88: Check the words you know and trace.

4 Think Look, read, and match.

1 

Where's your aunt?

2 

Where's your cousin?

3 

Where's your mom?

4 

Where are you?

a 

I'm in the yard.

b 

She's in the hallway.

c 

She's in the bathroom.

d 

He's in the bedroom.

5 About Me Draw yourself. Ask and answer with a friend.

Where are you?

I'm in ...

6 Listen and write the number.

1 

2 

3 

4 

5 

7 Draw the objects in the picture. Ask and answer.

Where's the ... ?

It's ... .

8 4.12 Listen and number.

9 What's missing? Look and draw. Then stick.

10 Trace the letters.

11 Listen and circle the *a* words.

4.15

1 

2 

3 

4 

What shape is it?

1 **Look and color the shapes.**

2 **What's next? Match, then draw and color the shapes.**

Evaluation

1 Read and trace. Then circle and say.

1 house

a 

b 

2 hallway

a 

b 

3 apartment

a 

b 

4 balcony

a 

b 

2 What's your favorite part? Use your stickers.

story | song | video

3 Puzzle Complete the color.

y_l_o_

Then go to page 93 and color the Unit 4 pieces.

Review Units 3 and 4

1 Write the words and match.

1	2	3	4	5	6	7	8	9	10	11	12	13	14	15	16	17
u	a	t	b	s	c	r	d	o	e	n	g	m	h	k	i	y

1 b r o t h e r
4 7 9 3 14 10 7

2 ___ ___ ___ ___ ___ ___ ___
15 16 3 6 14 10 11

3 ___ ___ ___ ___ ___ ___ ___
12 7 2 11 8 13 2

4 ___ ___ ___ ___
17 2 7 8

5 ___ ___ ___
8 2 8

6 ___ ___ ___ ___ ___
14 9 1 5 10

a 

b 

c 

d 

e 

f 

2 Read and match the questions with the answers.

1	Where's the computer?	c	a	She's in the living room.
2	Is that your cousin?	___	b	No, it isn't. It's my sister.
3	Who's that?	___	c	It's on the desk.
4	Where's your mom?	___	d	It's my sister.

3 Circle the correct words and write.

mom bedroom grandma ~~under~~

1

What's / (Where's) the doll?

It's __under__ the bed.

2

Who's / Where's this?

It's my ____________ .

3

Who / Where are you?

I'm in my ____________ .

4

Is that / Who's your aunt?

No, it isn't.

It's my ____________ .

5 My body

1 Read and circle the correct word.

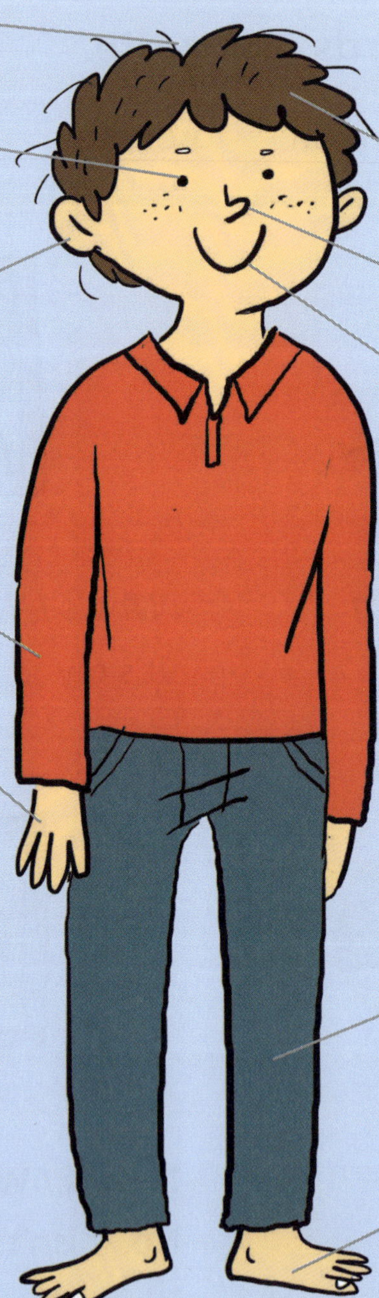

1 head / hand

2 eyes / arms

3 legs / ears

4 arms / feet

5 ears / hands

6 hair / mouth

7 nose / hair

8 head / mouth

9 legs / eyes

10 hands / feet

2 5.05 Listen and stick.

1

2

3

4

5

6

3 Look at the picture. Find and circle the words.

h	e	a	d	e	p	n
l	e	g	l	a	l	o
h	h	k	o	r	j	s
a	a	e	r	t	y	e
i	r	w	h	a	n	d
r	m	o	u	t	h	n
q	n	v	f	e	e	t

My picture dictionary Go to page 89: Check the words you know and trace.

4 5.08 Listen and check ✓.

5 Think What's different? Circle the word.

1

(eyes) / ears

2

feet / hands

3

legs / arms

4

mouth / nose

6 Look, read, and check ✓.

1

Do you have hair?

☐ Yes, I do. ☑ No, I don't.

2

Do you have two arms?

☐ Yes, I do. ☐ No, I don't.

3

Do you have four legs?

☐ Yes, I do. ☐ No, I don't.

4

Do you have one nose?

☐ Yes, I do. ☐ No, I don't.

7 About Me Draw a robot. Then complete the sentences.

I have ________________

______________________ .

I don't have ________________

______________________ .

8 5.11 Listen and check ✓.

1

2

3

4

9 What's missing? Look and draw. Then stick.

10 Trace the letters.

An iguana
with pink ink.

11 Listen and circle the *i* words.

1 

2 

3 

4 

What sense is it?

1 Look, read, and match.

1 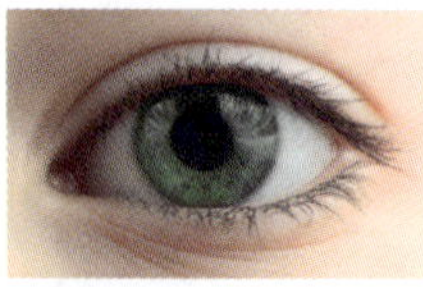

2 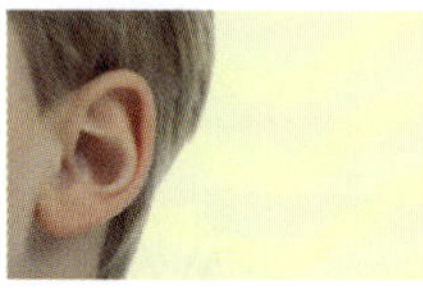

3 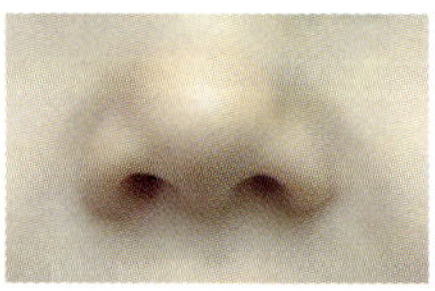

4 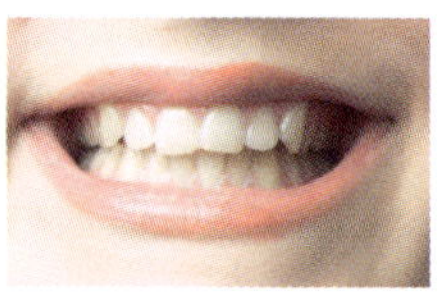

5 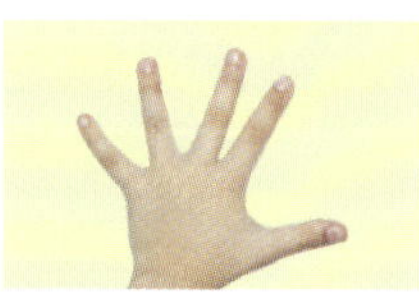

hearing

taste

sight

touch

smell

a 

b 

c 

d 

e 

2 Look and check ✓.

		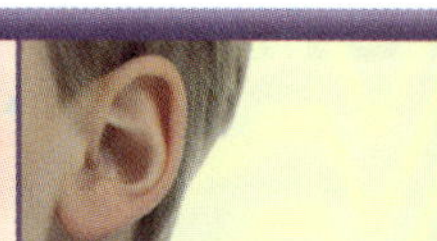	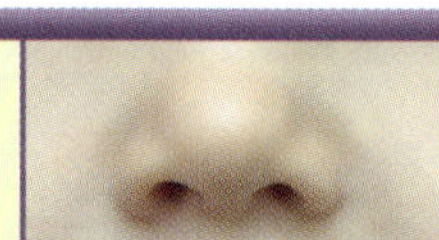	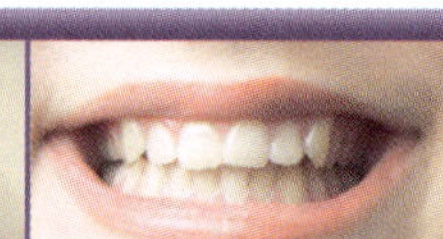	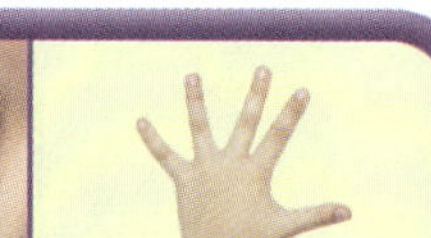
	✓				

Evaluation

1 Look, match, and trace. Then read and say.

head

feet

ears

nose

2 What's your favorite part? Use your stickers.

3 Puzzle Complete the color.

b_u_

Then go to page 93 and color the Unit 5 pieces.

6 Food

1 Look and write the word.

1  kmli — milk

2  pealp — ______

3  geg — ______

4  cehsee — ______

5  aewrt — ______

6  aaannb — ______

2 Complete the words and match.

1 juice 2 o_ange 3 b_ead 4 c_ick_n

a 

b 

c 

d 

3 Listen and stick.

1

2

3

4

4 Think Look and write the words.

~~cheese~~ an apple juice bread water
a banana an egg an orange chicken milk

We eat …

1 cheese
2 ______
3 ______
4 ______
5 ______
6 ______
7 ______

We drink …

1 ______
2 ______
3 ______

My picture dictionary → Go to page 90: Check the words you know and trace.

5 6.08 Listen and check ✓ or put an ✗.

1 			✓	✗
2 				
3 				
4 				

6 Look, read, and circle.

1 

I like / **(don't like)** juice.

2 

I **like** / **don't like** oranges.

3 

I **like** / **don't like** bread.

4 

I **like** / **don't like** water.

5 

I **like** / **don't like** apples.

6 

I **like** / **don't like** eggs.

7 Look, read, and check ✓.

1

Do you like bread?

☑ Yes, I do. ☐ No, I don't.

2

Do you like eggs?

☐ Yes, I do. ☐ No, I don't.

3

Do you like bananas?

☐ Yes, I do. ☐ No, I don't.

4

Do you like juice?

☐ Yes, I do. ☐ No, I don't.

8 About Me Look and answer the questions with *Yes, I do* or *No, I don't.*

1  Do you like chicken?

______________________________.

2  Do you like milk?

______________________________.

3  Do you like cheese?

______________________________.

4  Do you like bananas?

______________________________.

9 6.11 Listen, look, and match.

10 What's missing? Look and draw. Then stick.

I'm patient.

11 Trace the letters.

An elephant
with ten eggs.

12 Listen and circle the e words.

6.14

1 

2 

3 

4 

Where is food from?

1 Look and check ✓ or put an ✗.

Plants

 ✓

Animals

2 Look, read, and circle.

1 

(plant) / animal

2 

plant / animal

3 

plant / animal

4 

plant / animal

5 

plant / animal

6 

plant / animal

Evaluation

1 Look, match, and write. Then read and say.

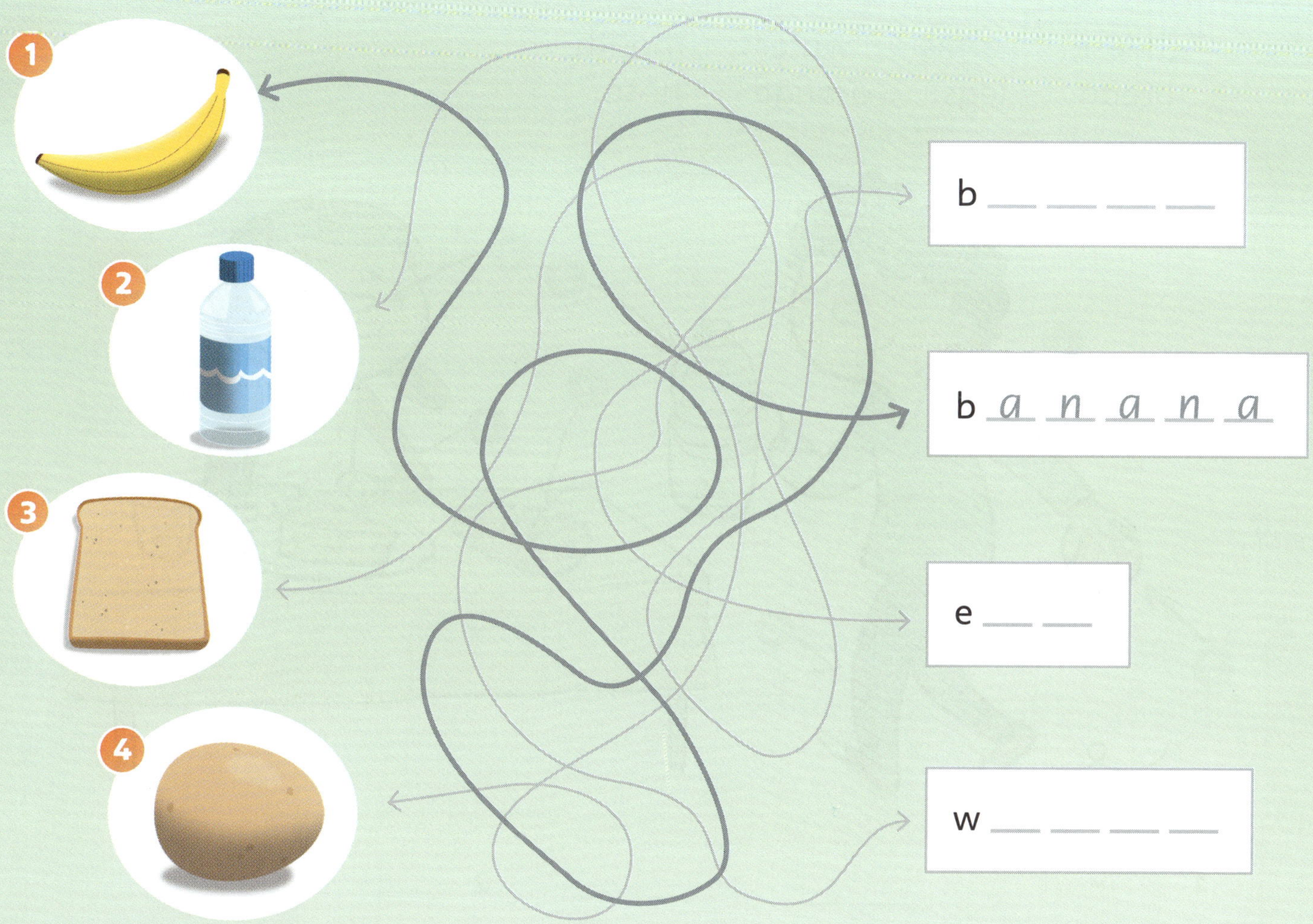

2 What's your favorite part? Use your stickers.

3 Puzzle Write the color.

p e u l r p ________

Then go to page 93 and color the Unit 6 pieces.

Review Units 5 and 6

1 Look and write.

cheese	~~arms~~	water	mouth
bread	legs	orange	nose

1 *arms* ____________ 2 ____________

3 ____________ 4 ____________

5 ____________ 6 ____________

7 ____________ 8 ____________

2 Read and match.

1	I like	a	like juice.
2	I have	b	two ears.
3	I don't	c	chicken.
4	I don't have	d	two heads.

3 Write the question. Then check ✓.

1

you / three / Do / have / hands / ?

Do you have three hands?

☐ Yes, I do. ☑ No, I don't.

2

like / eggs / you / Do / ?

____

☐ Yes, I do. ☐ No, I don't.

3

have / two / you / Do / ears / ?

____

☐ Yes, I do. ☐ No, I don't.

4

you / Do / milk / like / ?

____

☐ Yes, I do. ☐ No, I don't.

7 Actions

1 Look, read, and circle the word.

1

swim / **sing**

2

climb / paint

3

dance / draw

4

ride a bike / play soccer

2 Look at the pictures. Find and circle the words.

1

2

3

4

5

6

runswimjumppaintclimb**dance**

3 Listen and stick.

1

2

3

4

5

6

4 Read and circle the object.

1 dance

2 draw

3 sing

4 swim

My picture dictionary → Go to page 91: Check the words you know and trace.

5 7.08 Listen and circle the picture.

1

2

3

4

6 Look and write *can* or *can't*.

1 I *can* run. 2 I ________ draw.

3 I ________ climb. 4 I ________ dance.

7 Look, read, and check ✓.

1

Can you swim?

[ ] Yes, I can. [✓] No, I can't.

2

Can you jump?

[ ] Yes, I can. [ ] No, I can't.

3

Can you ride a bike?

[ ] Yes, I can. [ ] No, I can't.

4

Can you dance?

[ ] Yes, I can. [ ] No, I can't.

8 About Me Complete the chart. Ask three friends and check ✓.

Name			
1 *Me*			
2			
3			
4			

Can you sing?

Yes, I can. / No, I can't.

9 7.11 Listen and number.

a

b

c

d

e

f

1

10 What's missing? Look and draw. Then stick.

11 Trace the letters.

An umbrella
bird can jump.

12 Listen and circle the *u* words.

7.14

1 

2 

3 

4 

What's the number?

1 Think and write the answer. Then color.

1	1 + 1 =	2	red	2	2 + 4 =		blue
3	3 + 6 =		orange	4	10 − 2 =		purple
5	5 − 2 =		green	6	8 − 4 =		yellow

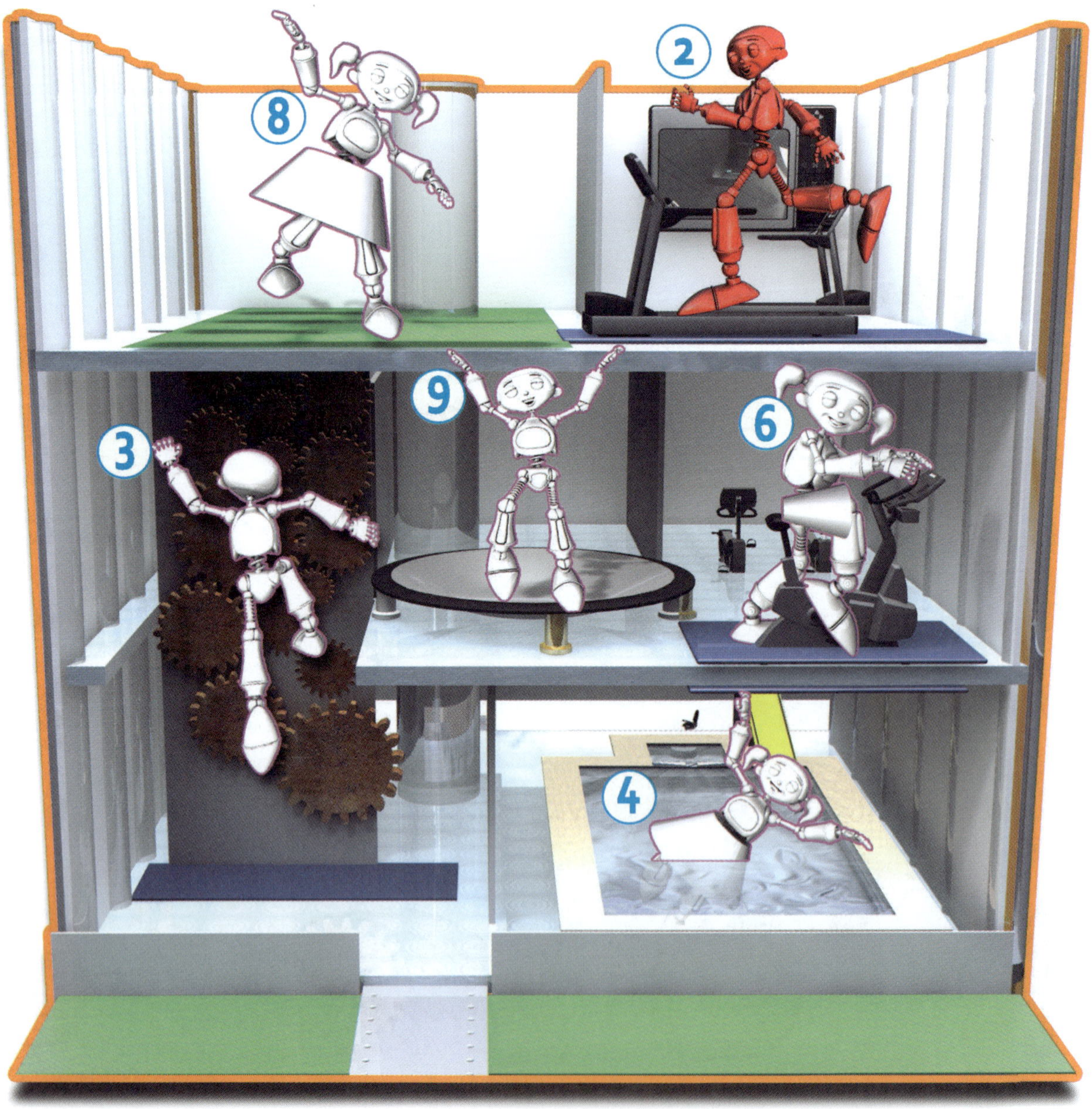

Evaluation

1 Look and write the words. Then read and say.

1 

r u n

2 

_ _ _ _ _

3 

_ _ _ _ _

4 

_ _ _ _

5 

_ _ _ _

6 

_ _ _ _

2 What's your favorite part? Use your stickers.

3 Puzzle Write the color.

a y r g ________

Then go to page 93 and color the Unit 7 pieces.

8 Animals

1 Look and match.

1 
2 
3 
4 

a crocodile   b giraffe   c spider   d elephant

2 Look and write the word.

1 

n l o i

lion

2 

b e r z a

______

3 

i d b r

______

4 

o i p h p

______

5 

m y o e k n

______

6 

e a k n s

______

3 Listen and stick.

8.05

1

2

3

4

5

6

4 Think Write the words. Circle the animals with four legs.

snake spider bird ~~zebra~~ elephant giraffe hippo lion

1

zebra

2

3

4

5
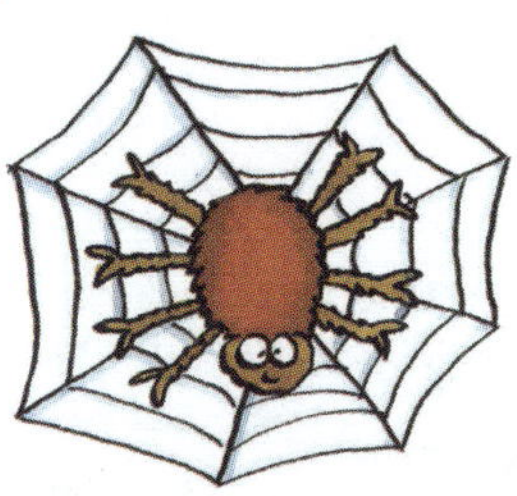

6

7

8

My picture dictionary → Go to page 92: Check the words you know and trace.

5 Look and match the opposites.

1 
big

a 
tall

2 
short

b 
small

3 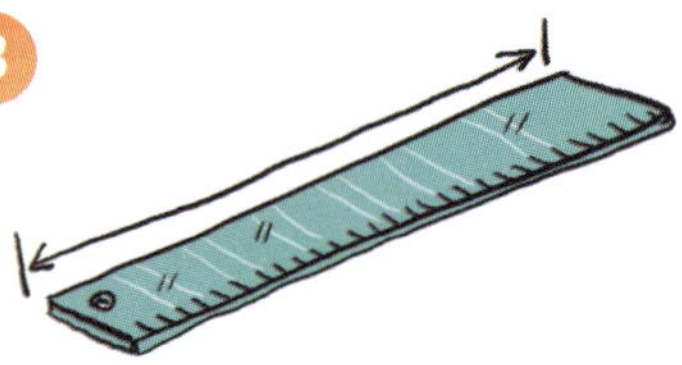
long

c 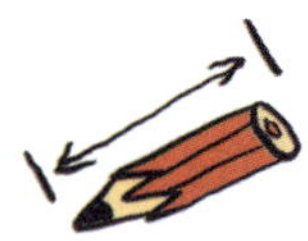
short

6 Look, read, and complete the sentences.

1 
Spiders are small.

2 
Monkeys are ______.

3 
Snakes are ______.

4 
Elephants are ______.

5 
Giraffes are ______.

6 
Baby crocodiles are ______.

7 Look and read. Circle the correct sentences.

1

Spiders have wings.

2

Elephants have long trunks.

3

Hippos have long necks.

4

Monkeys have long tails.

8 Look and write.

big teeth   long tails   ~~small wings~~   long necks   short legs

1 Birds have small wings.
2 Zebras have ______ ______.
3 Hippos have ______ ______.
4 Giraffes have ______ ______.
5 Birds have ______ ______.

9 About Me Ask and answer with a friend.

What are your favorite animals?

Elephants.

10 8.11 Listen and check ✓.

1

2

3

4

11 What's missing? Look and draw. Then stick.

12 Trace the letters.

An octopus in
an orange box.

13 8.14 Listen and circle the *o* words.

1 
2 
3 
4 

How do animals move?

1 Read and complete. Then number the pictures.

slither ~~walk~~ fly walk

1. An elephant can walk .
2. A snake can ________ .
3. A bird can ________ .
4. A giraffe can ________ .

a

b

c

d

2 Look at Activity 1 and circle the answers.

1. Can a snake fly? Yes, it can. / No, it can't.
2. Can an elephant walk? Yes, it can. / No, it can't.
3. Can a bird fly? Yes, it can. / No, it can't.
4. Can a giraffe slither? Yes, it can. / No, it can't.

Evaluation

1 Look and write the word. Then read and say.

1

z e b r a

2

_ _ _ _

3

_ _ _ _ _

4

_ _ _ _ _ _ _ _

5

_ _ _ _ _ _ _

6

_ _ _ _

2 What's your favorite part? Use your stickers.

3 Puzzle Write the color.

l c k a b ____________

Then go to page 93 and color the Unit 8 pieces.

Review Units 7 and 8

1 Look and write. Then draw number 9.

1 
2 
3 
4 

					9								
1				z	*e*	*b*	r	*a*					
2						a			o		c		r
3	s		a										
4		j											
5						i		p					
6						n		e					
7				o			e						
8		a		n									

5 
6 
7 
8 

9

2 Look and write.

soccer small long necks a bike ~~swim~~

1 Can you swim ?
2 Birds are ______ .
3 I can play ______ .
4 Giraffes have ______ .
5 I can't ride ______ .

3 Look, read, and circle the words.

1

Snakes / **Spiders** are long.

2

I **can** / **can't** sing.

3

Hippos **have** / **don't have** short tails.

4

I can **draw** / **dance**.

Hello!

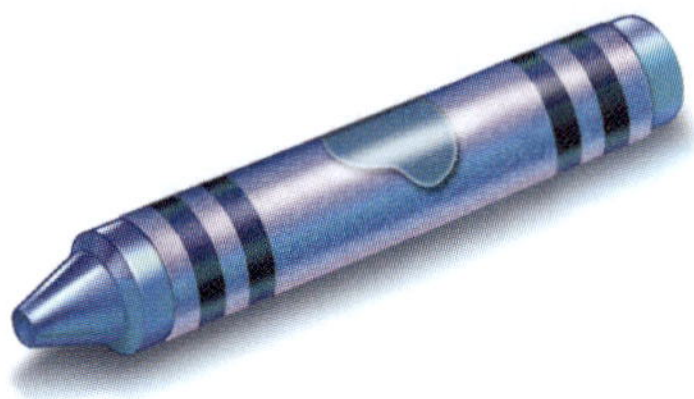

blue

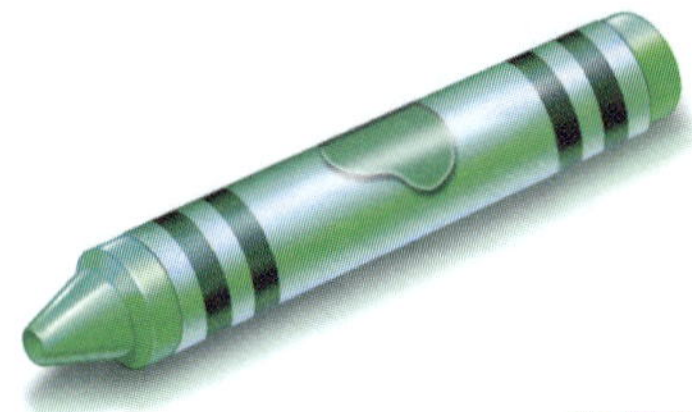

green

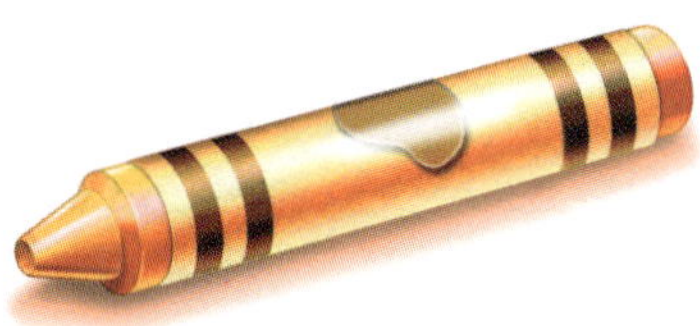

orange

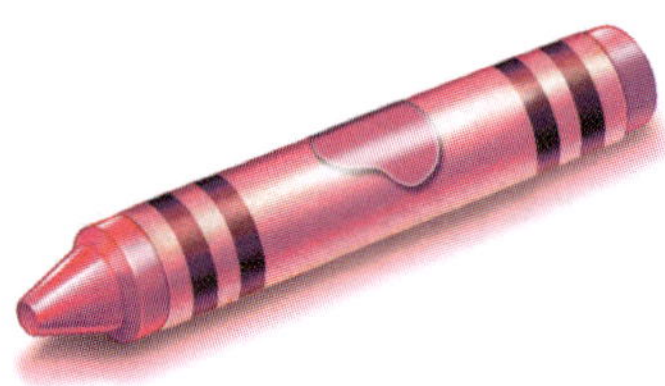

pink

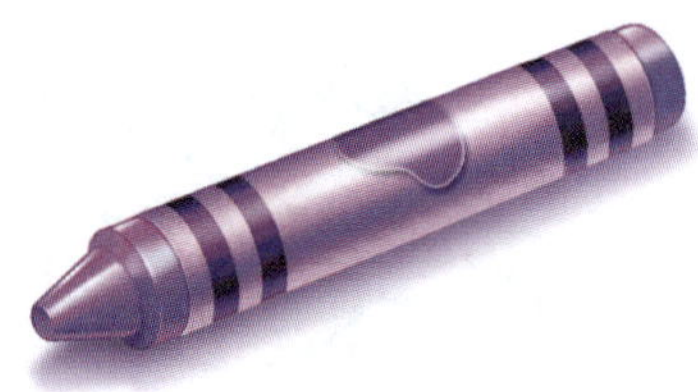

purple

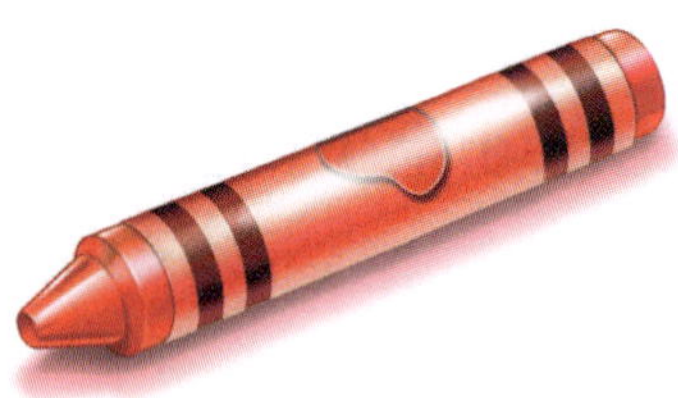

red

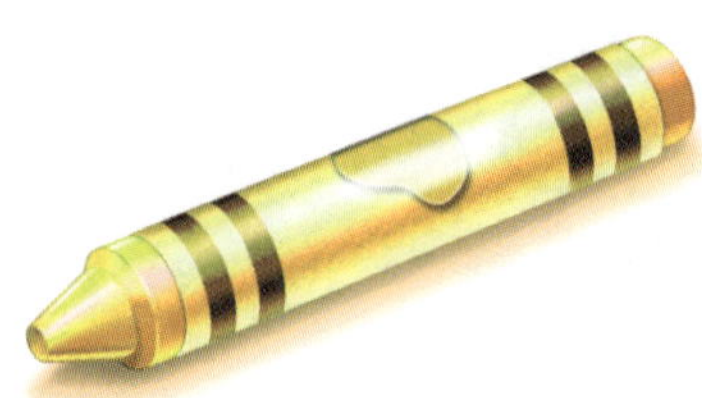

yellow

1 School

board

book

chair

desk

door

pen

pencil

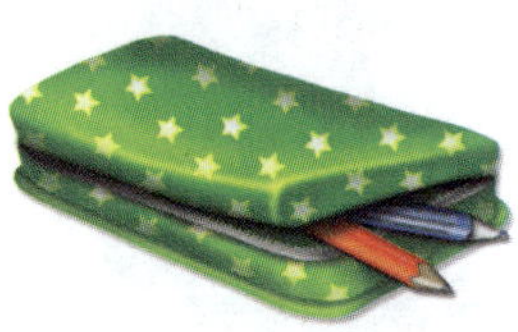

pencil case

eraser

window

2 Toys

✓ art set

☐ ball

☐ bike

☐ camera

☐ computer

☐ computer game

☐ doll

☐ kite

☐ robot

☐ teddy bear

3 Family

✓

aunt

brother

cousin

dad

grandma

grandpa

mom

sister

uncle

4 At home

balcony

bathroom

bedroom

dining room

apartment

yard

hallway

house

kitchen

living room

5 My body

☑ arms

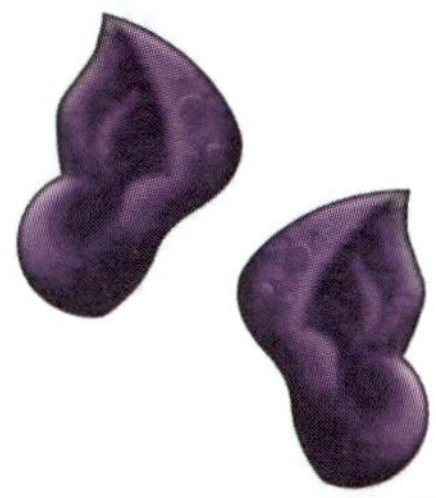

☐ ears

☐ eyes

☐ feet

☐ head

☐ hair

☐ hands

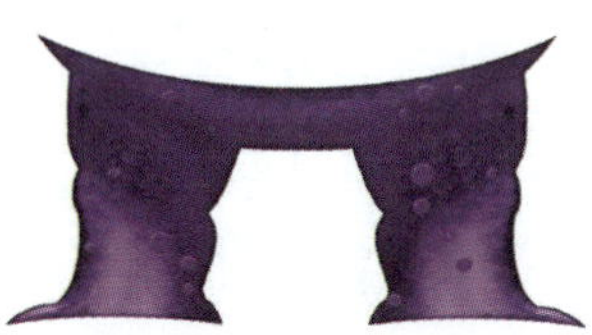

☐ legs

☐ mouth

☐ nose

6 Food

apple

banana

bread

cheese

chicken

egg

juice

milk

orange

water

7 Actions

climb

dance

draw

jump

paint

play soccer

ride a bike

run

sing

swim

8 Animals

bird

crocodile

elephant

giraffe

hippo

lion

monkey

snake

spider

zebra

My puzzle

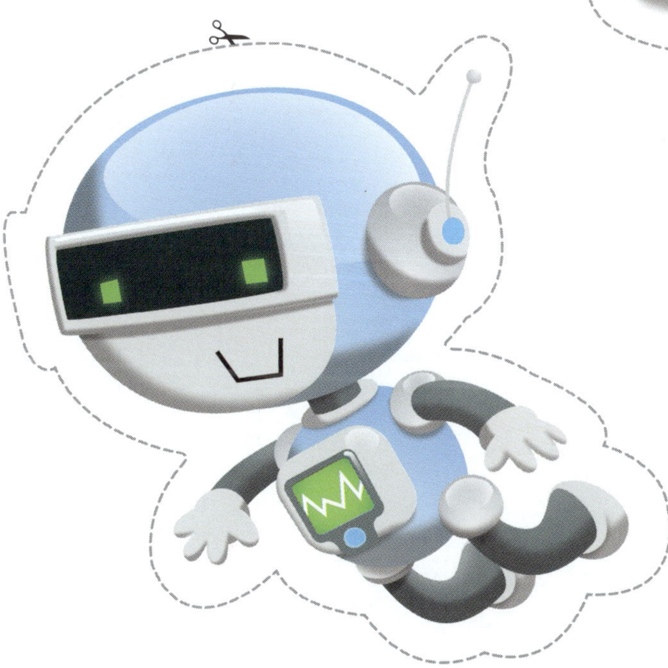

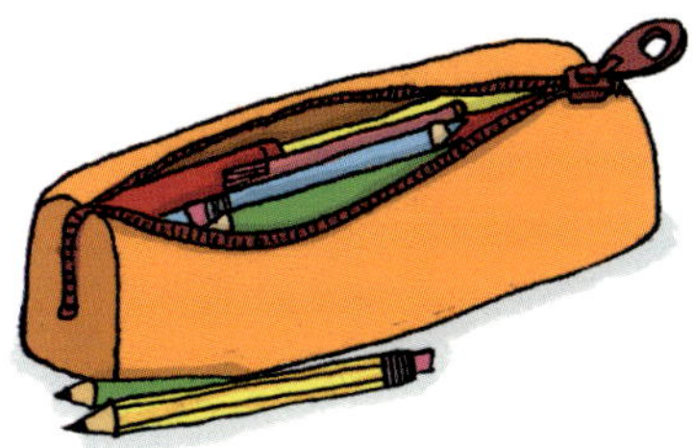